M000249172

Red, White, and Blue

Printed in Mexico

ISBN-13: 978-0-15-352716-6
ISBN-10: 0-15-352716-1

6 7 8 9 10   050   11 10 09 08

Harcourt
SCHOOL PUBLISHERS

Visit *The Learning Site!* www.harcourtschool.com

Our Country Begins

Many people worked hard for America's freedom. **Freedom** is the right to make choices.

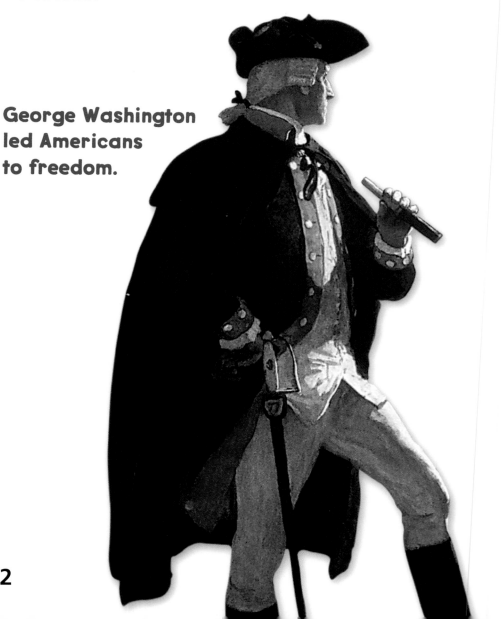

George Washington led Americans to freedom.

The Declaration of Independence and the Constitution are important American documents. Both papers tell about our freedom.

Reading Check (Focus Skill) **Main Idea and Details**
What documents tell of America's freedom?

The Declaration of Independence was signed in Independence Hall.

3

George Washington

He was a fair man. People liked him. They trusted him.

Time

1732
Born

1749
Starts making maps of land

Washington joined the army. He became a great leader. He led Americans.

1799
Died

1775
Becomes a leader in the army

1789
Becomes the first President of the United States

Learning About Freedom

People write to show how they feel. They write to share ideas. These writings were made long ago.

A page from John Adams's journal, 1776

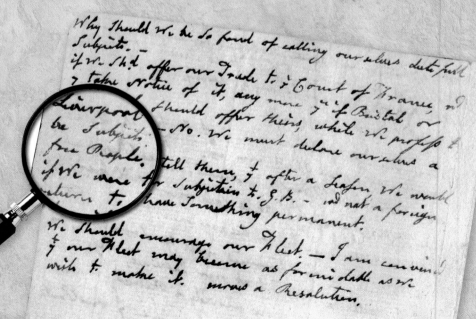

The Declaration of Independence

IN CONGRESS. JULY 4, 1776.

The unanimous Declaration of the thirteen united States of America,

1. What can you learn by reading a journal?

2. Look at the bottom of the Declaration of Independence. What do the names tell you?

I Pledge Allegiance

The American **flag** is a symbol of our country. Each morning we face the flag. Then we say the Pledge of Allegiance.

The 50 stars stand for the states in our country. The 13 stripes stand for the first 13 states.

The **Pledge** of Allegiance is a promise to respect the flag and our country.

 Reading Check Main Idea and Details

What is the Pledge of Allegiance?

American Symbols

The United States has many symbols. They stand for things important to the country.

The bald eagle is an American symbol.

Symbols can be places to visit. This kind of symbol is called a **landmark**.

Reading Check Main Idea and Details

What is a landmark?

Capitol

Holidays and Heroes

National holidays are special days. We remember important events and heroes of our country.

Fourth of July celebration

A **hero** is a brave or important person. Our country has many heroes. We honor them with holidays.

Reading Check **Main Idea and Details**

What is a hero?

Abraham Lincoln

Dr. Martin Luther King, Jr.

Activity I

Match the word to its meaning.

freedom   flag   pledge

landmark   hero   national holiday

1. a kind of promise
2. a brave or important person
3. the right people have to make their own choices
4. a piece of cloth that is a symbol
5. a place to visit
6. a day to honor a person or an event

Activity 2

Look at the list of words. Put the words in a chart like this one. Then use a dictionary. Learn what the words mean.

settler   colony   freedom

flag   pledge   landmark

hero   national holiday

	I Know	Sounds Familiar	Don't Know
settler	✓		
flag	✓		
colony			✓
hero		✓	

(Focus Skill) **Main Idea and Details** Why do we have national holidays?

1. **Vocabulary** Why do people visit a **landmark**?
2. Who was George Washington?
3. Why is the American flag important to us?

Activity

Draw a Picture Draw a picture of one of your heroes. Write a sentence telling about your picture.

Photo credits
Front Cover Ariel Skelley/CORBIS; 8 Harcourt; 9 Harcourt; 10 Tom and Pat Leeson; 11 Index Stock
Imagery; 13 (tl) Harcourt Index; (br) Library of Congress